Power Networking from the Inside Out

Where Your Career and Your Well-Being Meet

ADVANCE PRAISE FOR POWER NETWORKING FROM THE INSIDE OUT: WHERE YOUR CAREER AND YOUR WELL-BEING MEET

Networking is such an important skill to have in order to be successful in all aspects of life. The author explains and demonstrates it well through examples throughout the book. This book is a must-have for students and professionals who are looking to expand their circle of colleagues and career possibilities.

Elizabeth Cardoso, Ph.D.

CRC, Chair, Department of Educational Foundations & Counseling Program; Professor of Counseling Programs Hunter College-CUNY.

In "Power Networking from the Inside Out: Where Your Career and Your Well-Being Meet," author Valerie Lyons presents a truly unique, reciprocal approach to traditional networking concepts, by emphasizing self-care and empowerment and building mutually beneficial relationships with others. These ideas will enable the reader to approach the networking process from a totally positive and self-worth point of view, as opposed to the mindset of, "I need to meet someone who can help me get a job." This makes the text a must-read for recent college grads, career changers and anyone who is interested in the dynamics of the networking process. Additionally, the integrated and repeated exercise at the end of every chapter help reinforce the concepts covered and prepare the reader to develop the skills necessary to become a lifelong and true "Power Networker."

Ted Goldstein

Dean, Bachelor's Degree Program, Monroe College

I work in academia where networking is key. After 20 years in the field, I thought I knew all about networking, but Valerie Lyons' new book, "Power Networking from the Inside Out: Where Your Career and Your Well-Being Meet," gave me a perspective on this important social skill I never thought about. The book is insightful and resourceful with a touch of love and care. You really get a sense Valerie cares about your well-being to live your best life using the power of networking as a tool."

Marie C. Nazon, PhD, LMSW
Counseling faculty SEEK Department, The City College of New York, Fulbright Alumni

Valerie Lyons distinguishes for each individual, each partner, each associate, each business and each organization how all networking is not alike. "Power Networking from the Inside Out: Where Your Career and Your Well-Being Meet," carries the central purpose that those with whom we network benefit from our collaboration in at least as much measure as we may ourselves. It begins "from the inside out" through conscious listening to others first and self-care as both a listening and responsibility for enabling ourselves to be our best listeners and contributors to the world. Valerie has illuminated both a way of life and an essential focus for youth and adult development.

R. Lloyd Jaeger, ed.D
President of Learning & Leadership Services, LLC; lifelong educator including teacher, school administrator and Superintendent of Schools.

Unlike most networking books, "Power Networking from the Inside Out: Where Your Career and Your Well-Being Meet," by Valerie Lyons, is an insightful guide for creating and fostering relationships to help grow careers as well as navigate life paths. Valerie raises networking to a higher level by inviting the readers to reflect upon their goals and intentions. If you are looking for practical tips, you will get these while also exploring and building even deeper foundations for networking. Valerie does this by sharing wisdom and then concluding with thought-provoking questions at the end of each chapter, which allows each person to customize this information. This is a book to keep on your shelf or Kindle. I find myself returning to it periodically as a way to build mutually beneficial relationships throughout different phases in both my professional and personal life.

Elyssa Gersen-Thurman, LMHC, CRC
Director of Work Wellness & Connections to Care
The HOPE Program & Sustainable South Bronx

Power Networking from the Inside Out

*Where Your Career and
Your Well-Being Meet*

Valerie J. Lyons

Power Networking from the Inside Out: Where Your Career and Your Well-Being Meet

Copyright and Disclaimer

Photographer: Michael Crawford, MyPapa Photography, www.mypapa.zenfolio.com, 914-407-4590

Makeup Artist: Shakeya Sharice Wall, SimNala Atistry, 718-8643468, SimNalaArtistry@gmail.com

Dedication

I dedicate this book in memory and honor of two very important women in my life — my mother, Sylvia Viola Lyons, who lived a life grounded in joy, compassion and love, and my aunt, Dorothy Mae Nelson, a Creative who loved fashion, music and travel. Thank you, Mom and Aunt Dot, for loving me fully and gifting me with the well-rounded attributes of a Power Networker!

Acknowledgment

I would like to first thank Divya Parekh, my Book Coach, who supported me greatly throughout the process of writing this book from concept to the reality. Thank you, Divya, for your patience, expertise and commitment to see to my success! I would also like to thank Elsie Maio, my Business and Branding Coach, for helping me flesh out some of the major concepts in this book. Elise, you are an invaluable resource to me and I appreciate you more than you will ever know. Last but not least, I would like to thank my dear sister, Cheryl Baez, who so diligently and methodically assisted me with the editing of this book. Thank you, Cheryl, for always wanting the very best for me!

Contents

Foreword

When I look back over my career, I can honestly say that I never made the connection between networking and self-care. When I worked in the corporate world, my job was the priority and I did not take the best care of myself. As a result, my health took a back seat.

"Power Networking: Where Your Career and Your Well-Being Meet" provides readers with a roadmap that integrates self-care, networking and career advancement. Valerie and I are both blessed to be in the experts' industry sharing our experiences and skill sets with professionals. I have spent a great deal of time with Valerie supporting her with building her business and bringing her brand voice to the masses. I want to share some things I have learned about Valerie, the author.

Valerie is one of the most experienced, thoughtful and generous people I've had the pleasure to coach and befriend. Her talents and experiences are wide-ranging. She is what I would call "a modern leader." She is committed to supporting others and has dedicated the better part of her career to connecting people with job opportunities and influencers.

Valerie divulges insightful networking concepts and strategies which will help you learn the art of active listening, how to use social media as a networking tool, and how being of service naturally creates opportunities. This book will help you catapult from an average networker to a power networker and achieve your goals in your personal and professional life.

Both Valerie and I believe that the journey to mastery begins the moment you decide to commit to self-care and self-advancement.

Also, dear networker, keep working on realizing your dream. Never forget that joy, success, and advancement often come from what can feel like seemingly never-ending efforts, invested time, and resources. A step taken is one step less towards your goal achievement. Take the first step.

Divya Parekh

Business Leadership Coach and 8-Time #1 International Best Selling Author

"Networking Frees us up from the Myth that we Should only rely on Ourselves to Succeed in Life."

~Valerie J. Lyons

INTRODUCTION:
THE FOUNDATION
OF NETWORKING

Power networking is an "inside" and "outside" learning and growth process. With traditional networking, we often focus on the external actions such as updating our resume, creating a business card, and practicing our "elevator pitch." These accomplishments are indeed necessary to be a successful networker. However, networking success can't be achieved without the equally important "inside" actions. In fact, we sometimes neglect the critical inside or internal actions such as understanding and expanding our sense of self, placing a priority on ongoing self-assessment and personal development, powerfully and intentionally managing our self-care and seeing ourselves as contributors to the world. A chapter of this book is dedicated to self-care as I believe this is sorely missing from the lives of many who are seeking to build and/or expand their careers. I've come to realize that power networking is a form of self-care! Our opportunities for success dramatically increase and stress and fear significantly decreases when we invite others to support us and champion our dreams, wishes and desires. Over the last two years, I have shifted from being "career-driven" to "life-driven!" With this new mindset, I now see my career as an important part of my life but not my world!

1

My self-care fuels everything that I do!

Contrary to popular belief, networking is not a one-sided activity where the primary objective is to get something from someone. In fact, networking has as much to do with giving as receiving. It is within the act of giving that you receive unforeseeable rewards. There may not be an immediate "return on your investment" but it will surely come! An important question to ask is, "How can I be of service?"

At its core, networking is truly about building and nurturing meaningful and reciprocal relationships. I've come to know that for many, networking occurs as stressful, uncomfortable and a chore. I wrote this book to bring freedom and ease to the art of networking.

Your success in developing strong reciprocal relationships will be fostered by the empowering way in which you see yourself as competent, courageous and clear. However, you will only be able to see yourself through this powerful lens if you: understand who you are, have clearly identified your goals/vision for your life, are intentional about managing your health and wellness and have fine-tuned the tools you need to get the work done. Whether our connection is solely through your reading of this book or whether you choose to follow up on this purchase by working with me on a one-to-one or group basis via my career empowerment coaching practice, I am committed to helping you reach your goals. I am passionate about helping others achieve their dreams!

Throughout the following chapters of "Power Networking from the Inside Out: Where Your Career and Your Well-Being Meet," I will challenge you to reflect and take action on both the inside and outside work necessary to be a "Power Networker!" I hope to empower you to think about networking in a new way that leads you to take action that propels you toward success!

After each chapter, I invite you to acknowledge yourself and celebrate your accomplishments. I am on a journey of embracing internal validation vs. relying on others to validate me. My desire is to heighten your level of self-efficacy while encouraging you to enhance and expand your relationships with others.

"Get Clear, Declare your Vision and Share."

~Valerie J. Lyons

MY NETWORKING JOURNEY

People don't believe me when I tell them that I am a "recovering" shy person. But it's true! I overcame my shyness by taking small steps to improve my level of self-confidence. Early in my career, I had a dynamic supervisor, Dr. Lisa Wyatt. Lisa was extremely bright, poised, engaging and energetic. I was in awe of her ability to attract people and maintain their interest. I carefully took note of her demeanor, her language, her disposition, even her professional attire. She encouraged me to take more risks by increasing my level of visibility within the organization. Through being asked and at times even pushed to make public presentations on her behalf, I gained confidence in talking to large groups of people. It took practice, practice, and even more practice! It wasn't easy but I was determined to conquer my fear of public speaking despite the self-doubts and my internal dialogue shouting in my ears, "Valerie, you cannot do this. You won't be able to deliver this information in a cohesive way. Nobody wants to listen to what you have to say."

Over time, I came to recognize that the more prepared I was, the more comfortable I became with public speaking. Being prepared requires that I get a good night's rest, take the necessary time to review my material, meditate, pray, and maybe most importantly, learn to embrace my unique style and way of being. When I finally realized that I didn't have to be just like my supervisor to be an effective public speaker, I truly had an "aha" moment!

This early experience served as a foundation for me to successfully build strong and long-lasting relationships. I now see myself as a "Power Networker!" I am no longer afraid to introduce myself to people and engage them in a conversation. I no longer believe in the concept of "stranger" as I see us all as being connected. I know that there is nothing between myself and someone else. If there is a perceived barrier, I put it there! When we choose to be vulnerable and share deeply with one another, we get to see how connected we really are! My objective is to be inquisitive, learn more about the person of interest and identify their needs.

I remember landing one of my first contracts with a not-for-profit agency. I had worked with the president of the agency many years ago. When I contacted her to schedule a meeting, my goal was to reestablish our relationship, fill her in on what had been happening in my life and determine if there was a particular need that I could fill within her organization. As it turned out, her agency had a number of volunteer programs that were fairly new and she hired me to analyze and evaluate the programs and suggest recommendations on how to establish best practices. I secured this contract through my networking efforts and meeting the needs of the employer. This was a very gratifying and confidence-building experience.

When I secured my current job as an advisor for the graduate programs in counseling at Hunter College, it was a newly created position that I learned about through a colleague. What makes this position particularly important to me is that it is a position I declared for myself before it showed up. I got clear that my strengths and gifts are teaching, leadership development, mentoring, coaching and training. I declared that I

was seeking a job where my colleagues were loving, supportive and competent. This job encompasses everything that I
asked for. In my work as a coach, I talk about the power of
your word and invite my clients to speak what they want (not
what they don't want) into existence; I express my gratitude
for this job every day! As an added blessing, I was recently
offered a promotion! I plan to create a seminar titled "How
to Secure a Promotion Without Asking for It!"

YOUR POWER NETWORKING JOURNEY

Reflection:

How can you use what you've learned in this chapter to move out of your comfort zone and take an action that will expand your self-confidence, skill set and career opportunities? Hint: You can request support from a friend, colleague, family member to assist you!

_____

_____

_____

_____

_____

_____

_____

_____

_____

_____

_____

_____

_____

_____

_____

_____

_____

_____

_____

_____

Action Steps:

List 1 or 2 action steps you intend to take starting today.

_____

_____

_____

_____

_____

_____

_____

_____

_____

_____

_____

_____

_____

_____

_____

_____

_____

_____

_____

_____

_____

_____

_____

_____

_____

_____

Celebration:

Book a spa treatment! Self-care is self-love. Whether it's a hand massage, facial or full-body massage, do something that's relaxing and nurturing. I collaborate with Denise Hanney, CEO/Founder of the Spa Expectations Corporation, for many of my networking events. I am committed to integrate self-care in my message of career empowerment and women empowerment!

How will you celebrate?

_____
_____
_____
_____
_____
_____
_____
_____
_____
_____
_____
_____
_____
_____
_____
_____
_____
_____
_____

"You Can't Put a Price Tag on Your Peace of Mind."

~Valerie J. Lyons

WHAT IS NETWORKING?

We are networking even when we are not consciously aware of it. Whether we are seeking employment, looking for a good doctor, building a business or working toward an academic degree, we have an opportunity to build relationships and give of ourselves in our efforts to achieve a desired outcome.

Networking can be defined in a variety of ways....

Dictionary.com

A supportive system of sharing information and services among individuals and groups having a common interest.

Wikipedia

Business networking is a socioeconomic activity by which groups of like-minded business people recognize, create, or act upon business opportunities. A business network is a type of social network whose reason for existing is business activity. There are several prominent business networking organizations that create models of networking activity that, when followed, allow the businessperson to build new business relationships and generate business opportunities at the same time.

Valerie J. Lyons

Power Networking is grounded in intention and a commitment to serve. It is the ability to build mutually beneficial relationships with individuals and/or groups with the goal of enriching the personal and professional lives of others while achieving one's own goal or dream. Power networking skills can be used to secure employment, advance in your career, expand your social circle or to create an online presence. Power Networking is an expression of love, community and gratitude. and manifests itself as a co-created miracle for yourself and others.

So, the million-dollar question is "What does networking mean to you?" For me, networking is sharing my gifts, talents, skills and resources to enhance the lives of others. It's also listening for opportunities to expand my social and professional network as well as potential opportunities to build my coaching, workshop facilitation and public speaking practice.

You may be saying to yourself:

- "I'm shy."

- "I am uncomfortable with introducing myself to new people."

- "I don't have anything interesting to say."

- "Nobody wants to hear what I have to say."

- "Networking is a waste of time."

- "I feel awkward when I try to network."

- "Networking takes too much effort."

These are all very common thoughts and beliefs that people have about networking and there's absolutely nothing wrong with any of it! However, it's important to note that just because you have these thoughts about yourself and others doesn't mean any of these thoughts are true! One of the biggest steps to take as a networker is to get out of your head and into the world. Having conversations with others, listening for what the other person is interested in and committed to will have you engaging in a conversation that focuses more on the other and less on you! Most people enjoy talking about themselves and they appreciate others who are genuinely interested in getting to know them.

Listening is a big part of networking and it is an action that is not emphasized enough. As a Power Networker, you are listening for:

- What interests, motivates and inspires the other person.

- How you can meet a need that is either said or unsaid.

- How that person is feeling and what they are experiencing in the moment.

- How you can encourage and empower the individual.

When I am having a conversation with another human being, I listen for the possibility and opportunity to create something new and exciting for myself, someone I know or for them! This is what I mean when I refer to in my definition of networking, "enriching the personal and professional lives of others."

YOUR POWER NETWORKING JOURNEY

Reflection:

How can you use what you've learned in this chapter to enhance and/or expand a new way to approach networking?

_____

_____

_____

_____

_____

_____

_____

_____

_____

_____

_____

_____

_____

_____

_____

_____

_____

_____

_____

_____

_____

_____

Action Steps:

List 1 or 2 action steps you intend to take starting today.

_____

_____

_____

_____

_____

_____

_____

_____

_____

_____

_____

_____

_____

_____

_____

_____

_____

_____

_____

_____

_____

_____

_____

Celebration:

Plan a trip that has been on your "bucket list"!

When I booked my trip to England to visit my brother and his wife, it had such an amazing impact on our relationship! Although I had valid reasons why it had taken me so long to make the trip, my not seeing him in his new environment left him feeling disappointed and frustrated! I'm so excited to be off to England for the holidays!

How will you celebrate?

_____

_____

_____

_____

_____

_____

_____

_____

_____

_____

_____

_____

_____

_____

_____

_____

_____

"*If you Really want to Know your Strengths, Reach out to Someone you Trust and ask them to Tell you your Gifts and Believe it.*"

~ *Valerie J. Lyons*

WHO NETWORKS?
WHO DOESN'T?

Y ou may be asking yourself, "Can I really be a Power Networker?" Take a minute and reflect on the questions below:

- Are you a student with a brief work history who is embarking upon a brand new career and have big dreams?

- Have you been working in an industry that you like, yet find yourself in a rut and desire more?

- Are you changing careers and it feels like you are starting over again and don't know where to begin?

- Do you describe yourself as an introvert and don't believe you can initiate a conversation with someone you do not know?

- Are you reluctant to request support?

- Are you concerned that an employer is going to prefer hiring someone who has a stronger work history than you have?

- Do you believe that you don't know the "right" people

to assist you in your job search?

If any of theses scenarios resonate with you, keep reading. This chapter is for you!

If you are entering an industry and have little to no prior work experience, let me remind you of what you do have!

You have fresh eyes

You bring a new, fresh perspective to an organization which may help to distinguish you from someone else who has been with the same company for many years. You may be able to identify organizational strengths or gaps in services that are not apparent to more senior staff members who, rather than see the need for change, believe a particular system should stay in place because "it's always been done that way."

You are eager

You are eager to get your foot in the door and prove how valuable you are. You bring a definite sense of excitement, urgency and energy!

You are open to growth

While you may not have an extensive work history in your chosen career, you have the opportunity to present yourself as someone who can follow directions and is a quick learner.

You have more work-related experience and skills than you think

Your work experience includes paid employment, internships, as well as volunteer and life experiences. For instance, if you have ever faced a challenge in your life and have overcome it, this example of resilience and steadfast determination can prove to be a powerful demonstration of your commitment to see a situation through from start to finish. Are you tech savvy? Have you traveled and been exposed to different cultures? Are you a member of a fraternity or sorority? Have you joined school clubs or professional organizations? What about community service? Continue to think of how your life experiences translate into marketable skills.

You absolutely do have contacts. Your network is bigger than you think and includes:

- Fellow classmates
- Professors
- Colleagues
- Members of your professional organization
- Members of your spiritual or religious community
- Family
- Friends
- Neighbors

If you have a strong work history, there is a good possibility you also have a strong work ethic. You know what it means to be a team player, get to work on time, manage office politics, lead by example, bring out the best in others and negotiate the work environment.

YOUR POWER NETWORKING JOURNEY

Reflection:

What are the personal and professional attributes that have you stand out from others?

_____

_____

_____

_____

_____

_____

_____

_____

_____

_____

_____

_____

_____

_____

_____

_____

_____

_____

_____

_____

_____

_____

_____

Action Steps:

List 1 or 2 action steps you intend to take starting today.

_____

_____

_____

_____

_____

_____

_____

_____

_____

_____

_____

_____

_____

_____

_____

_____

_____

_____

_____

_____

_____

_____

_____

Celebration:

Create time in your schedule to see friends and family. I created a "Friend Marathon of Love!" I set aside two days to meet with, call or text as many loved ones as possible! It was a beautiful experience to connect with people I had not seen or heard from in a long time!

How will you celebrate?

_____

_____

_____

_____

_____

_____

_____

_____

_____

_____

_____

_____

_____

_____

_____

_____

_____

_____

_____

_____

"The Misperception is that we are all Strangers; The Miracle is we are all Connected."

~Valerie J. Lyons

HOW DO WE NETWORK?

Networking begins with you! We all know the saying: "It's not what you know, but who you know." I have modified this slogan by adding "It's not just what you know and who you know, but **WHO YOU ARE**." Do you feel optimistic and hopeful? Do you feel confident? Do you have an "elevator pitch" or, as I call it, a "passion pitch" memorized that you can deliver naturally in conversation? Do you feel prepared to present your qualifications? Do you have a "professional persona"? Do you have a business card or a "calling card"? Do you have the technical and interpersonal skills to not only get the job, but keep the job?

I often hear people speak of the "law of attraction," which is the belief that like attracts like and that by focusing on positive or negative thoughts, one can bring about positive or negative results (Wikipedia). However, I believe we have to take it even a step further and consider the "law of manifestation," which according to the late Dr. Wayne Dyer is as follows: "We manifest into our lives **who we are, not what we want**." The "law of manifestation" supports the notion that one must be prepared, emotionally, physically, spiritually and psychologically to be an effective networker and to attract individuals and opportunities that we desire.

I also want to bring your attention to the opportunity to net-

29

work within your current work environment. You may have a job that you enjoy, yet you may feel stuck in your current position. You may have an interest in advancing within your organization but are not clear as to what steps to take. Oftentimes we neglect building a network within our organization. Building an internal network keeps you in the know; exposes you to new opportunities, situations and projects; and therefore can support you in your commitment to advance in your career.

Building a **Success Team** can help you strengthen your level of confidence, provide you with the support you need to stay motivated, and help you sharpen your networking skills. Most importantly, your **Success Team** can hold you accountable. Some potential people for your team are already within your immediate reach (e.g., friends, family members, neighbors, colleagues, classmates, professors, house of worship parishioners, etc.).

Members of your **Success Team** can fulfill the following roles:

- **The Coach Mentor:** This is someone who has reached the level of success you aspire to have. You can learn from their success as well as their mistakes. Heed your "Coach Mentor's" wisdom and experience. The "Coach Mentor" also keeps you abreast of trends inside and outside of your chosen field and keeps current on industry topics that you may find interesting. This person provides support and guidance around important life decisions and offers an objective perspective.

- **The Champion:** This is someone who unapologetically sings your praises in your presence as well as in your absence.

- **The Power Supporter:** This is someone who has access to people, resources and information. As soon as they come across something of interest to you, they reach out to you to keep you informed. Your "Power Supporter" is also great at uncovering unique ways to make linkages as well as finding resources and opportunities that most people would overlook.

- **The Inspirer:** This person motivates you to "think big" by how their life has unfolded. The "Inspirer" can help you envision an actual plan to reach your goal. One personal encounter with your "Inspirer" can powerfully change the direction of your life. This is the person to call when you want to brainstorm for new ideas. Without judgment, your "Inspirer" is focused on helping you flesh out your dreams in high definition, by often seeing beyond what may be the obvious.

- **The Mentee:** This is someone whom you can mentor, support and guide. One of the best ways to tell that you understand something is to be able to explain it to someone else. And sometimes, one of the best motivators for pushing through obstacles and hardships is knowing that someone is watching.

- **The Accountability Partner:** This is someone who holds you to your word and follows up with you to ensure that you are following through on said tasks. Your "Accountability Partner" is willing to give of their time and energy. This person will help you keep it real by not knocking your dreams, but rather, challenge you to identify the action steps needed to make your dream happen.

You may find that one person can fulfill multiple roles. For example, your "Coach Mentor" may also serve as your "Inspirer" and "Power Supporter."

YOUR POWER NETWORKING JOURNEY

Reflection:

Who are the members of your Success Team?

_____

_____

_____

_____

_____

_____

_____

_____

_____

_____

_____

_____

_____

_____

_____

_____

_____

_____

_____

_____

_____

_____

_____

_____

Action Steps:

List 1 or 2 action steps you intend to take starting today.

_____

_____

_____

_____

_____

_____

_____

_____

_____

_____

_____

_____

_____

_____

_____

_____

_____

_____

_____

_____

_____

_____

_____

Celebration:

Contribute to others. Contribute to a cause you believe in, sponsor someone's participation in a conference or serve as a mentor. I give to others regularly and I'm blessed tenfold!

How will you celebrate?

_____

_____

_____

_____

_____

_____

_____

_____

_____

_____

_____

_____

_____

_____

_____

_____

_____

_____

_____

_____

_____

"Being of Service is the Gift that Keeps on Giving."

~Valerie J. Lyons

Here is a special gift for you! The
ABC's of Powernetworking. Click here:
http://www.valeriejlyonsenterprises.com/

THE POWER OF PRO BONO

I am frequently asked to conduct presentations for groups who do not have the budget to pay for my services. When I choose to offer my services at no charge, I apply the same degree of dedication, preparation, passion and effort as I would for a job for which I am being paid. I address the audience as I would clients who paid top dollar to hire me and I interact with them in a way that says, "I'm competent, clear and engaging; you are getting your money's worth and then some!" I use pro-bono jobs as an opportunity to be of service, broaden my network and market my services.

For those readers who are new to entrepreneurship, I recommend that you be strategic in your approach to pro-bono work. Taking on engagements for no charge can help you hone your craft and enhance your credibility while building a powerful following of potential clients. However, you also have to balance your innate nature to give with how many pro-bono jobs you can *afford* to take on, given the investment of time and other resources that each opportunity requires.

Many years ago I interviewed for a position within a not-for-profit that provides services for female survivors of domestic violence. Although I did not get the job, I did get invited to be a keynote speaker for two of their events. Several months after that, I was asked to do yet another pro-bono presentation for this agency; I stated that I would love to provide the service, however, I would be seeking a fee or honorarium. I was told that there were no funds available in the budget to pay me so I declined the job. As much as I loved working for this agency, I determined that my pro-bono days with them had come to an end. However, soon after, I received a call from my contact at this same agency and she shared that she now had a budget and asked if I was available. I gave her my usual consultant rate and I am confirmed to conduct a seminar.

In another example, I was asked to conduct a pro-bono presentation for a group of SEEK (Search for Education, Elevation and Knowledge) counselors who work in the CUNY system. I facilitated a one-hour presentation, "Counselor Wellness: Caring for the Caregiver." Afterwards, one of the participants in this session recommended me to a faculty member at John Jay College as they were seeking someone to facilitate a staff retreat. I secured the contract with John Jay College and got very positive feedback on my presentation and how I kept the participants engaged. This in turn resulted in a referral to conduct a staff retreat for City College! So, you can see from this experience how one pro-bono event led to two paid consultant contracts! Power Networking is the gift that keeps on giving! That's what I'm talking about!

YOUR POWER NETWORKING JOURNEY

Reflection:

In what ways can you use pro-bono opportunities to expand your business and/or career options?

_____

_____

_____

_____

_____

_____

_____

_____

_____

_____

_____

_____

_____

_____

_____

_____

_____

_____

_____

_____

_____

_____

_____

Action Steps:

List 1 or 2 action steps you intend to take starting today.

_____
_____
_____
_____
_____
_____
_____
_____
_____
_____
_____
_____
_____
_____
_____
_____
_____
_____
_____
_____
_____
_____
_____
_____
_____

Celebration:

Take an action that you are resisting. Let this be an action that you may have some fear around taking, but that you truly believe will give you freedom. During one of the transformational leadership programs that I participated in, I took on doing the things that I was the most confronted by — doing the things that scared me the most — like saying yes to being a Team Leader without having it all figured out! This willingness to step outside of my comfort zone to transform my fears had me fear less! Now I feel like I can take on the world!

How will you celebrate?

_____

_____

_____

_____

_____

_____

_____

_____

_____

_____

_____

_____

_____

_____

"Power Networking Creates Connections that Last a Lifetime."

~Valerie J. Lyons

BEYOND THE
BUSINESS CARD

I n my early days as a Power Networker, I advised students who were scheduled to attend a conference, networking event or professional training to "collect" business cards from at least three people they did not know. What I since learned is that effective networking is much more than securing business cards. Prior to stepping foot inside a networking event, it's important to first prepare for the event. For example, it makes a difference to know something about the event organizer, understand the purpose of the event, and take great strides to show up as your best. This kind of preparation elevates your self-esteem and self-confidence. This "behind the scenes" work leaves you competent and clear about your passion and the value that you can add to an employer's mission and vision. In addition to asking for a business card from someone of influence, you would want to first engage in a brief (no more than 5 minutes) conversation to build rapport. Be in a state of inquiry; ask them what's important to them and listen for their passion and purpose. Make sure that on the back of each business card you write points of reference to assist you with remembering who the person is and why you want to follow up with them. You may even want to download a business card scanner that allows you to send text messages, make phone calls or email right from the app!

You can even take a picture of the business card and e-mail it to yourself as a reminder to make contact with the individual of interest. I remember attending a professional conference some years ago and my mantra was *"Go Beyond the Business Card; Secure a Meeting."* I was prepared to not only get a potential employer's business card but also to let individuals know that I was seeking work as a consultant and that I would follow up with them to schedule a meeting. As it turned out, I made quite a few promising contacts. My marketing coach assisted me in the preparation of a follow-up e-mail which highlighted my skill set and areas of expertise. I also forwarded my CV. I subsequently heard back from a CEO of a large behavioral health care organization who made arrangements for me to meet with two of his senior leaders. While I didn't secure a gig, this experience continues to be a clear reminder of just how powerful the business card exchange can be if you are intentional about your purpose and committed to following up!

Divya, my business coach, encourages me to use my books as an enhanced business card as it is a very effective marketing and promotional tool. I have indeed done just that and, as a result, I have secured a number of speaking engagements.

Here is a resource that will give you examples of creative business cards: https://www.boredpanda.com/creative-business-card-designs/

YOUR POWER NETWORKING JOURNEY

Reflection:

What are some new ways of looking at how you can promote or market your services, skill set, or business?

_____
_____
_____
_____
_____
_____
_____
_____
_____
_____
_____
_____
_____
_____
_____
_____
_____
_____
_____
_____
_____
_____
_____

Action Steps:

List 1 or 2 action steps you intend to take starting today.

_____

_____

_____

_____

_____

_____

_____

_____

_____

_____

_____

_____

_____

_____

_____

_____

_____

_____

_____

_____

_____

_____

_____

_____

_____

Celebration:

Post your accomplishments on social media. Self-acknowledgment is key to building confidence and strengthening self-esteem. When you acknowledge yourself, you make room for others to acknowledge you. See how many likes and comments you get. I believe that people are rooting for me...because they are! Allow people to root for you!

How will you celebrate?

_____

_____

_____

_____

_____

_____

_____

_____

_____

_____

_____

_____

_____

_____

_____

_____

_____

_____

"There is No Such Thing as Work/Life Balance. All we Have is Our Life! Create a Beautiful Life and an Awesome Career will Show Up."

~Valerie J. Lyons

POWER NETWORKING:
A COMMITMENT
TO SELF-CARE

I am blessed to have an extensive network of amazing friends, clients, business partners and other personal and professional contacts. For most of my professional life, my gift of networking has led to success in growing my career, expanding my knowledge and skill set while helping others do the same. I absolutely love being of service and it brings me great joy to support others in creating their career!

In my early 50s, I began investing in my personal development. It soon became very clear to me that I had placed a considerable amount of energy furthering my career and paid little attention to my self-care. Although I was happy with my work life, my personal life suffered. I was facing some difficult challenges in my marriage and I used food for comfort and as a way to avoid dealing with the conflicts in my relationship. The fact that I exercised sporadically and did not stay on top of my required medical exams just exacerbated my health problems.

Through the transformational work I've been doing with several programs, I gained the courage to confront my self-destructive behaviors and recognize that I had the power to choose my well-being! When I chose to make self-care my number one priority, my network expanded dramatically to include leaders and people of influence from a variety of disciplines. I now integrate my commitment to self-care within my networking events.

I recently held an event themed "Self-Care: Love in Action." The event included an interactive discussion on how self-care is either present or missing in our lives. We identified actions to expand and enhance our lives physically, emotionally, spiritually, sexually, financially and professionally. Featured speakers included: Michelle Zaylar, a Love Coach; Elizabeth Madison, a Registered Dietician who has a faith-based weight loss management program; and Emara Grainger, a Personal Trainer and "Afrobics" instructor. This was a wonderful opportunity for participants to share their victories and challenges with managing their self-care while meeting professionals available to support them in pursuing their wellness goals. I am so excited about upcoming plans to create a holistic women's empowerment event in 2019! This retreat will include a special focus on self-care and self-love! Stay tuned!

I'm using my commitment to self-care to create holistic networking events that focus on specialized topics such as: career empowerment, financial planning, book coaching, fitness and health wellness, entrepreneurial business building, beauty/hair care, and spa services. I'm excited and proud to know experts in these industries. I truly understand that taking a holistic approach to self-care is the foundation of my success and I am committed to encouraging others to make their well-being a priority!

I have a dear friend and colleague, Elyssa Gersen-Thurman, Director of Work Wellness & Connections to Care with the Hope Program. Elyssa is the author of a health and wellness blog.

Check out her blog. Here is the link!: http://hellowellmeaning.tumblr.com/

YOUR POWER NETWORKING JOURNEY

Reflection:

What does self-care mean to you?

_____

_____

_____

_____

_____

_____

_____

_____

_____

_____

_____

_____

_____

_____

_____

_____

_____

_____

_____

_____

_____

_____

_____

_____

Action Steps:

List 1 or 2 action steps you intend to take starting today.

_____

_____

_____

_____

_____

_____

_____

_____

_____

_____

_____

_____

_____

_____

_____

_____

_____

_____

_____

_____

_____

_____

_____

_____

_____

_____

Celebration:

Honor your Word. Keep a promise you made to yourself. I made a promise to myself that I would buy myself flowers on a regular basis! This promise has supported my commitment to create home as sanctuary. What promise will you keep? How will you honor your word?

How will you celebrate?

"You can't get Fired From your Purpose."

~Valerie J. Lyons

SOCIAL MEDIA: AN EFFECTIVE POWER NETWORKING TOOL

S ocial media offers job seekers, professionals, and entrepreneurs a multitude of opportunities including but not limited to:

- Connecting with influencers in your chosen field

- Expanding your visibility to create an online presence

- Building your brand

- Identifying needed resources

- Expanding your social and professional circle

- Identifying career advancement opportunities

Trying to determine which social media platforms to use can be a daunting task. It helps to thoroughly research the role and function of the various social media platforms that you believe will support your goals. Through the process of experimentation, you will determine which platform works best for you. You also need to determine how much time you can realistically allocate to interacting on social media. I encourage you to be patient with yourself as you work though this initial phase of developing a social media strategy.

In this chapter I will highlight a select number of social media platforms that can support you with networking, building your brand, advancing in your career, and organizing your job search or business projects. I will give you a brief description of each tool and share with you how I've utilized these platforms to create my online presence, advance in my career and promote my business.

When interacting with people on social media, get to know them before making a request and listen for ways in which you can be of service. The social media arena continues to grow in really creative ways and I am committed to growing with it so I am better equipped to assess the various options and leverage those that work best for me. As I have become more comfortable and proficient in using social media, I have seen an increase in the number of people who view me as an influencer in the networking and empowerment space. This has resulted in an increase in my ability to earn money doing the things I love. I am committed to building my skill set in the use of social media to expand my business, that's for sure! There is so much to learn and it's very exciting! So here we go!

Creating Content

Since so much of social media is visual, you can unleash your creativity by creating your own graphics to enhance your texts, posts, blogs, photos, videos, etc. Websites like Canva and PicMonkey offer social media post templates and stock images ready for personalizing, which can also be helpful if you want to experiment with varying approaches to engage your target audience.

https://www.picmonkey.com

One word of caution — before you use any web tools, check the user's policy.

I enjoy using Canva, a tool that allows you to create beautifully designed posts. The site offers over 60,000+ templates; some are at a minimal cost and a large majority of the templates are free! **https://www.canva.com**

Become a Subject Matter Expert While Building Your Network

One of the largest professional online networking sites is LinkedIn. LinkedIn allows you to create a virtual resume, connect with influencers in your field of interest and post personal viewpoints about specific topic areas. I enjoy reviewing my LinkedIn page to learn about trends in the workforce development field. I've also found great articles on networking, job seeking and interview tips.

A couple of years ago I thought it would be a great learning experience to utilize technology to expand the career empowerment services that I provide. I created a closed group on LinkedIn titled "Job Success From the Inside Out," an online job club. Group members used the group to post their job-seeking activities; share resources; express their thoughts, fears and concerns about the job-seeking process; and support each other by giving feedback and encouragement to one another. Ultimately, everyone in the group found employment!

Here is my LinkedIn page https://www.linkedin.com/in/valeriejlyons/

Here is what two "Job Success From the Inside Out" group members had to say:

Participating in Valerie's LinkedIn Job Club was right on time for me. I had not been unemployed for 20 years and it helped bring me up to speed on how to powerfully leverage my professional network. I learned, and utilized, practical tips designed for those of us who are challenged by 'the ask' and in fact I landed a job.

Therese Salmon, PMP, Project Manager

When I suddenly lost my job of 5 years, and it was suggested to me by Valerie that I join her online support group, "Job Success From the Inside Out," I had mixed feelings about participating in the group. I knew full well that the group was designed to give support to the members who were job seeking, however I wondered if I could ever obtain employment again, and I also feared that I would be the last one in the group to do so. To my surprise, the group gave me the fortitude to continue with my job search. As we started to update each other with upcoming interview dates, each of us ultimately began to feel more confident about our skills and abilities and I regained my self-esteem. Eventually, we were each able to share that – "Hey, I have been given an offer!" Thank you, Valerie, and thanks to the group, I fulfilled my desire to earn my master's degree and I secured my current dream job!

Vanessa Scholack, ACCES VR Counselor

Strengthen Connections, Expand Your Knowledge Base, and Share Your Business Values

Social media vehicles such as Instagram, Twitter, Facebook, Pinterest and podcasts allow individuals seeking new connections to access customers, gather needed information and join targeted affinity groups.

Facebook is the largest global social media platform, with over 2 billion users as of 2018. There is great potential to connect and share your work globally by listing your business on a public page. Here is the link to my Facebook page:

https://www.facebook.com/valerie.lyons.56

Instagram is a visual platform where you can showcase your work and art. The platform also offers story posts that are available for 24 hours before disappearing.

Here are the links to my Instagram pages:

https://www.intstagram.com/valjlyons

https://www.intstagram.com/thepowernetworker

I use my Facebook and Instagram pages to post upcoming events and motivational messages, and introduce my followers to the interesting people that I meet. I've also used social media to promote the work, accomplishments and projects of others. There are people who follow me on Instagram who are not my "friends" on Facebook. By using both platforms, I continue to strengthen my reach.

Creating a Twitter page will allow you access to ongoing discussions with people of personal and professional interest. Searching hashtags on Twitter will lead you to threads of tweets on almost any topic and conversation. Nothing should stop you from asking a question about what someone tweeted or even commenting on a tweet that resonated with you.

Pinterest is a social network that allows users to visually share and discover new interests by posting images or videos to their boards. I have found Pinterest to be extremely resourceful for my personal and professional interests. I have used Pinterest for everything from finding networking tips, inspirational messages that I've integrated within my women empowerment seminars, to finding delicious vegan recipes and new hairstyles. If you have not explored this social media platform, I recommend that you do so! It's a lot of fun and slightly addictive!

Check me out on Pinterest: https//www.pinterest.com/valeriejlyonsenterprises

Podcasts are another way for you to increase your knowledge on networking, job seeking, advancing in your career and branding. I listen to Career Cloud Radio and have gained timely tips on various topics of interest such as resume preparation, salary negotiation, interviewing skills, and how to use LinkedIn effectively. Below is a link to seven podcasts that can help you find employment.

https://www.glassdoor.com/blog/podcasts-help-you-find-a-job/

Organizing Work and/or Business Related Projects

Trello is a free project management website that functions like a digital vision board. Although Trello is not a social media tool, you can use it to help you organize your social media activity and keep track of your job search and networking experiences. You can assign due dates to tasks to keep yourself on track, add partners if you're working on projects with others and keep all your tasks in one place. There's room for media if you want to create visual boards or attach photos to projects.

I use Trello in the planning of my women empowerment and networking events. This tool helps me to organize all the moving parts that go into event planning (i.e. logistics, marketing the event, the content of my presentation, etc.) as well as map out a well thought out social media strategy.

https://trello.com

Divya, my book coach, recently introduced me to WomElle (https://www.womelle.com) and I am proud to be a Founding Member. WomElle is a community that brings women across the globe together to share ideas and provide guidance that allows women to achieve their collective and individual goals.

A thoughtful, engaging social media plan is key to building your networking community. Check out these links below:

https://sproutsocial.com/insights/social-media-marketing-strategy/

https://sproutsocial.com/insights/social-media-editorial-calendar/

Don't Forget to Take Care of Yourself!

As previously mentioned, creating an online presence can be a daunting and time-consuming task. It is easy to become saturated by the profiles, opinions and updating timelines, so logging off now and then can help you to recharge. Sometimes great ideas reveal themselves when you're relaxed and in tune with yourself and your environment. So, allocate dedicated time for social media and make sure you also take some downtime to do the things that bring you joy!

YOUR POWER NETWORKING JOURNEY

Reflection:

How can your use of social media enhance your professional and personal life?

_____

_____

_____

_____

_____

_____

_____

_____

_____

_____

_____

_____

_____

_____

_____

_____

_____

_____

_____

_____

_____

_____

Action Step 1:

Research social media platforms and identify two platforms relevant for your power networking and career building goals.

_____

_____

Action Step 2:

Create your profile on two social media platforms of your choice. Write down your plan to expand your online presence on these platforms.

_____

_____

_____

_____

_____

_____

_____

_____

_____

_____

_____

_____

_____

_____

_____

_____

Celebration:

Find a place of natural beauty near your home: I recently visited a dear friend, Elsie Maio, Founder/CEO of Humanity Inc./SoulBranding Institute. Elise lives near a body of water and walking with her along the beach created a sense of peace, serenity, calm and centeredness for me. I was reminded of the amazing healing powers of water!

How will you celebrate?

_____

_____

_____

_____

_____

_____

_____

_____

_____

_____

_____

_____

_____

_____

_____

_____

_____

_____

_____

"A Power Networker Networks for All!"

~Valerie J. Lyons

FOLLOW THROUGH, FOLLOW UP AND GIVE THANKS

The networking process does not end when you achieve your desired outcome. When people refer you to their contacts, it's important to recognize that they are placing a great deal of trust and faith in you. You are representing them and your actions are either going to be perceived as a positive or poor reflection of them. Respect and honor the support that others give you and your referrals will grow. I also want to stress how important it is for *you* to be mindful of who *you* refer to others. Your credibility and reputation can be tarnished by recommending people who are not aligned with your values or work ethic. You want to recommend people who you know well and who you believe can truly excel in the endeavor that they are pursuing.

Remember to show your appreciation to individuals who have helped you achieve your goals. Send an e-mail, call, or surprise them and go "old school" with a handwritten note. Updating your referral source on the outcome of their job lead and personally thanking them for their support goes a long way toward maintaining this valuable relationship. I recently sent an e-mail to a client thanking her for the opportunity to conduct a retreat for her staff. My client's response was so favorable that I asked her permission to post it on the testimonial page of my website!

YOUR POWER NETWORKING JOURNEY

Reflection:

Think of all the people who have given you access to a resource or opportunity that made a difference in your life. How can you acknowledge them?

_____
_____
_____
_____
_____
_____
_____
_____
_____
_____
_____
_____
_____
_____
_____
_____
_____
_____
_____
_____
_____

Action Steps:

List 1 or 2 action steps you intend to take starting today.

_____

_____

_____

_____

_____

_____

_____

_____

_____

_____

_____

_____

_____

_____

_____

_____

_____

_____

_____

_____

_____

_____

_____

_____

_____

_____

Celebration:

Purge and Declutter. When I took on ensuring that my space was clutter free, creativity, freedom and ease showed up powerfully! Clean your home. Throw out that paper that seems to multiply when you are not looking. Shred old bills, donate books and give away clothes that you are no longer wearing.

How will you celebrate?

_____

_____

_____

_____

_____

_____

_____

_____

_____

_____

_____

_____

_____

_____

_____

_____

_____

_____

_____

_____

_____

"Having it all Doesn't Mean Doing it All."

~Valerie J. Lyons

WHERE TO NETWORK

In addition to traditional networking outlets such as social events, professional workshops, conferences, volunteer activities, social media platforms such as LinkedIn, and informational interviews, you should be prepared to articulate your qualifications, dreams and goals anywhere and at any time. You never know when and where your dream opportunity will present itself! Some years ago, I participated in a workshop highlighting an amazing program called "*Recovery Through Entrepreneurship.*" This program (which is now a not-for-profit organization), created and managed by the late Dr. Harry Wexler, Dr. Gerald Melnick, Jordan Wexler and Adam Gunther, provides career empowerment opportunities for individuals formerly involved in the criminal justice system and folks in recovery from substance use. Through the use of a digital platform, this innovative program offers individuals the tools they need to learn, build, and develop projects on their own so they can start to think, act, and behave like effective entrepreneurs. I was so thrilled to learn about this exciting program that from my seat in the audience, I exclaimed, "I want in!" I have been promoting the organization ever since. We've collaborated on a couple of specialized entrepreneurial type trainings for Certified Rehabilitation Counselors who are interested in starting a private practice, and I was hired to do consultant work for the organization.

I often find myself on the subway or shopping in a grocery or department store with the expectation of meeting people who are seeking something: happiness, a fulfilling career, meaningful relationships, a deeper sense of purpose, etc. I ask myself, "Does he look approachable? Might she be interested in the services I have to offer?" More often than not, I take the plunge and ask, "Do you love what you do?" or "What are you committed to?" These powerful questions serve as a way to engage people, inform them of my coaching/consulting practice and provide me with the information I need to link them with contacts in my network!

If you're somewhat introverted, shy, or don't consider yourself a natural networker, keep these things in mind:

- Other people want to network too.

- Practice helps to build your confidence.

- Social media platforms such as LinkedIn, Facebook and Twitter are great networking tools. The key is to network where people in your field are showing up.

- It is far less pressure and much more enjoyable to think of networking as an opportunity to connect with another individual rather than to have an expectation of getting something.

I invite you to liberate yourself from labels! We label ourselves and others all the time. We say we are shy, direct, introverted, extroverted, etc. All that does is limit us to behave and act in a certain way in every situation that we encounter. Labeling ourselves as "something" puts us in a box. It does not free us up to explore what it means to be outgoing, or what it means to be reserved. What it means to be reflective or what it means to be adventurous. Life is not about being any particular way. Life is about experiencing your full self in a space of joy, fulfillment and peace. Getting to where it is that you want to be may in fact have you push yourself outside your comfort zone, because after all, that is where transformation lives!

YOUR POWER NETWORKING JOURNEY

Reflection:

How can you expand the variety of settings where you might typically network?

_____

_____

_____

_____

_____

_____

_____

_____

_____

_____

_____

_____

_____

_____

_____

_____

_____

_____

_____

_____

_____

_____

_____

Action Steps:

List 1 or 2 action steps you intend to take starting today.

_____

_____

_____

_____

_____

_____

_____

_____

_____

_____

_____

_____

_____

_____

_____

_____

_____

_____

_____

_____

_____

_____

_____

_____

_____

Celebration:

Physically restore yourself. Go on a one-hour walk, take a Zumba class, run, jump Double Dutch! I enjoy walking and I love the idea of functional walking. I walk to the subway to go to work and I love the idea that I'm getting my exercise in the morning, clearing my head for the day and starting the day off doing something for myself!

How will you celebrate?

_____

_____

_____

_____

_____

_____

_____

_____

_____

_____

_____

_____

_____

_____

_____

_____

_____

_____

_____

_____

"If you want to Increase your Level of Self-Confidence and Self-Esteem, be a Contribution to Others."

~Valerie J. Lyons

WORDS FROM THE INSIDE

I hope you were inspired by what you've read and that it propels you to take action! My desire is that you now have a fresh new perspective about networking. Remember, networking is from the inside out. It begins with owning your power, managing your health and well-being, acknowledging that your fear does not have to stop you from moving forward and taking comfort in understanding that we are all connected and inherently want to support one another. It's about you presenting yourself as an invaluable resource to others. It also helps to have a supportive team of individuals to guide you in this process and hold you accountable. Ultimately, giving with an unconditional heart will result in reaching your goals!

If you are interested in utilizing my services, please feel free to contact me at powernetworker1@gmail.com. I specialize in career and women empowerment, working with career changers, students and clinicians. Until then, I will leave you with a poem that I wrote titled "*Living In Your Glow.*" May these words be a source of encouragement and affirmation as you pursue your dreams!

LIVING IN YOUR GLOW

Just in case you didn't know

We all have the glow

That inner spark that lights the fire in your heart

That rhythm in your flow

Align with your spirit and

Release your glory

Stop second-guessing yourself

Let the world know your story

Cherish the best of you

The imperfections too

Embrace fully who you are

Take hold of your power

and

Walk into your dream

Valerie J. Lyons

WHAT'S NEXT?

Congratulations on finishing "Power Networking from the Inside Out: Where Your Career and Well-Being Meet." As a special gift from me to you, I'm offering a 45-minute strategy session to help you take what you have learned in this book to the next level ... a dynamic and immediate action plan! Additionally, I will send you a personalized power networking checklist! Contact me at powernetworker1@gmail.com to register for this gift valued at $200.00! Thank you!

ABOUT THE AUTHOR

Valerie, CPC, CRC, LMHC is a passionate Career Empowerment Coach, Women Empowerment Facilitator and Power Networker with over 20 years of experience positively impacting and teaching others how to be the leaders of their own lives and careers. Valerie is a dynamic speaker and expert group facilitator who works with individuals and groups to provide them with practical and systematic approaches to actualize their life goals and objectives.

Valerie is committed to transforming the act of networking from what many experience as uncomfortable and intimidating to a holistic, healing and loving approach. Valerie wholeheartedly believes in the power of "We" and the innate desire we each have to be a contribution to one another.

Valerie is the Founder of Valerie J. Lyons Enterprises, a coaching and consultant practice. Her clients include colleges, not for profit organizations, religious institutions and professional associations. She also serves as the Advisor for the Graduate Programs in Counseling within Hunter College's School of Education.

Made in the USA
Columbia, SC
11 April 2019